Walking with Jesus
in Strange Places

theology MY

John
Swinton

Walking with Jesus
in Strange Places

Fortress Press
Minneapolis

WALKING WITH JESUS IN STRANGE PLACES

Originally published by Darton, Longman, and
Todd London, UK

Print ISBN: 978-1-5064-8453-2
eBook ISBN: 978-1-5064-8454-9

Cover design: Kristin Miller

Contents

1
Finding my vocation(s)

I NEVER PLANNED on being a theologian. What I really wanted to do was become a rock star. Indeed, I spent a good deal of the first 33 years of my life trying to achieve that goal. As I write I am preparing to release my first album, so you never know. In the end I became a theologian, and I am very happy with that as an outcome for my life. But how I got here is interesting. When I look back over the past 40 years or so of my life, it's difficult to see the connections between what I thought I would be and do back then, and what I have ended up being and doing. I have never really had a career plan or even a life plan. I don't mean that I never plan, I just mean that I rarely sit down and think: 'What am I going to do with the rest of my life.' I probably plan more now that I am a bit older and beginning to sense my mortality, but when I was younger, I tended just to go with the flow of life and see what happened. When I left school at 17, I had no clue what I wanted to do. I went to a rough school where, with one or two notable exceptions, university wasn't considered to be a viable option. Those who did express the desire to study further tended to be ridiculed and abused psychologically and physically for having ideas above their station. Expectations were low, and we all managed to meet them. For me, university was never an option. It was much more fun to develop a healthy scepticism towards all things educational and all people who liked such things. Which probably explains my school exam results.

My first job was as a marine scientist which is hilarious when you consider my obvious challenge when it comes to anything to do with numbers and statistics. I am almost completely right brained, which is great if you are a musician, a poet (and perhaps a theologian), but less helpful for a scientist. The mismatch between the job and me was quickly exposed, and I was sacked within my first year. The question 'What will I do?' was on my mind and filled the horizons of my anxious parents. I took a job as a van driver. I loved that job! I just got up in the morning, did my job and went home again at night. No worries, and some lovely Northeast countryside to drive around. It was bliss. Not much money but zero work stress. But I knew I couldn't do that forever, so I had to think about what I wanted to do on a more permanent basis. One of my best friends at the time had just become a mental health nurse so I thought: 'Why not try that?' I did. And I loved it! I had wandered into what turned out to be my vocation. Strangely enough, although it was never on my mind, this was the time when I began my formation as a theologian.

I trained originally in mental health and then retrained in the area of what was then called mental deficiency, and which has gone through a variety of names since – mental retardation, mental handicap, learning disabilities, intellectual disability. The current term of choice seems to be 'intellectual disability', although some in the UK still retain the term learning disability, a term which in the USA relates to things like dyslexia (a language processing disorder), dysgraphia (difficulty in converting thoughts into writing or drawing) and dyscalculia (problems related to mathematical calculations). It's complicated. These kinds of name changes make me a little suspicious of the politics of naming. The phenomenon remains the same, but the name changes with the politics, assumptions, values and attitudes prevalent at particular periods of time and across cultures. Disability is much more than something that is contained within your own body. It is also determined and defined by the place in which your body is located. But more on that later.

The formation of a theologian

These years of nursing were deeply formative *for* me and *of* me. When you spend time with people who see and encounter the world differently you begin to realise that the way you thought the world was may not be the only way in which the world can be seen. I

12

listened to people living with schizophrenia tell me their stories of hearing voices and the ways in which that experience brought them deep distress, but sometimes happiness and companionship. Listening to such experiences I began to realise how much my understanding of schizophrenia had been shaped and formed, not by listening carefully to what people were saying, but by making certain assumptions based on what I had been taught (my clinical formation) and what culture assumed (my cultural formation).

Whilst my clinical formation taught me to look for signs and symptoms and to frame people's experiences of illness in these terms, lurking below this perspective was a cultural worldview that, via the press or TV (no social media back then!), almost exclusively framed schizophrenia in terms that were profoundly negative: 'split personality!', 'violent and dangerous!', 'beyond understanding!', 'completely distant from the world'. And yet, when I spent time with people living with schizophrenia, I came to know them by their names and not their diagnoses. When that revelation occurred, the cultural veil was ruptured, and I was opened up to new realities and fresh possibilities. In coming to see *people,* rather than diagnoses, I began to understand schizophrenia differently. I started to recognise the difference between *treating* someone who has schizophrenia, and *being with* John, Brenda and Jean as they went through deeply troublesome experiences. Even then, key questions began to form in my mind. 'Why do we stigmatise people in such ways?' 'Why are people with this condition so lonely?' 'Why can't they find friends?' 'Is it "them" or is it "us" the problem lies with?' *'Where is God in the midst of such distress?'*

Similarly, as I spent time with people living with depression, I began to realise just how complex and painful depression is. Like many others, I used the language of depression as if it were just some kind of derivation of sadness. I'd talk about the 'Monday morning blues', or how depressed I was because my car was playing up. But as I spent time with people living with depression, I saw how weak and thin such language was. I remember one woman describing her depression as a pit that she tumbled into. When she was down there, she could look up and occasionally she would see flashes of light, but for most of the time there was nothing. Just darkness. She tried to climb out, but the walls of the pit were too slippery. All she could do was wait to be rescued. For her this meant therapy and medication alongside of people to sit with her in the darkness. Even when she was well, she said she spent her life walking round the edge of the abyss of depression, knowing that at any moment she could fall back in. That is a far cry from the 'Monday morning blues'. When I heard her story and other stories like hers, my whole perspective on depression changed, as did my understanding of why it might be that someone may not want to live with such experiences. My naïve assumptions about God always being with us began to shake a little. 'Does God really abandon us in the way that people are telling me?' 'What does it mean that Jesus felt abandoned on the cross?' *'Why does God allow such deep suffering to occur?'*

Finding the questions

My first day in the wards as a nurse was an absolute nightmare! I was nineteen and had little life experience. I was a failed scientist and a disenfranchised truck driver who really wanted to be a musician. I turned up on the ward without a clue as to what to do. In my life as a scientist, I caught and measured lobsters. If the patients had been lobsters, I would have had more of a clue what to do. But they weren't. They were people living with dementia. The ward was mayhem. People were shouting, running around with a sad, lost look in their eyes. And that was just the staff! The smell of urine and faeces was terrible. Everything seemed to be completely out of control. And in a sense, it was. Back then the idea that you could actually help people with dementia to live constructive lives was just beginning to emerge. We definitely cared, but society hadn't yet moved on to a place where dementia was something that contained dignity and hope as well as sadness and suffering. But even with the best of intentions, it is a serious challenge to try to keep safe, feed and clean 40 patients when you have a staff of three. We'd march people into the dayroom and line them up to watch children's programmes on television. There was little stimulation and very little meaningful relational contact. Of course, back then, implicitly and explicitly, we assumed that the people we were caring for were somehow lost and unreachable. It's not that we didn't want to offer better care, or that we didn't have the intuition that the people we were caring for had more to offer. We wanted to do more, but how could we when we had so many patients, so few staff and so little time?

But even then, in the midst of the turmoil, questions were beginning to bubble up within me. 'It can't be right that we have to hold people down to feed them. Is there not a kinder and more gentle way?' After all its somebody's mum or dad that we are dealing with. 'Why is it that when people with dementia hear music it brings out a response and an awareness that simply does not occur in other circumstances?' 'Why does someone sometimes find a great peace when I simply hold their hand?' *'Where is God in the midst of such lives?'*

Finally, in my years working with people with intellectual disabilities, particularly those who had little or no ability to communicate verbally, I was always struck by the strangeness of lives that weren't dependent on words. What must it be like to be in the world and unable to articulate that 'being?' As a 'good' Presbyterian, I 'knew' that everything religious comes through words. The word is preached, the Word is passed on through words, and even our salvation is dependent on saying the right words and believing the right things. And yet here was a group of human beings, loved by God and without any possibility of ever having or using words. I was disturbed. Unsettled. I remember sitting with one young man – Robert – as he died. He had no words. He had no way of accessing God in the ways that religion often demands of us. As I watched him take his last breath, I prayed and wondered, 'Would Jesus really reject Robert from heaven because he wasn't able to proclaim his name? That can't be right.' In the presence of the end of this tiny life, some deep theological questions began to emerge that challenged my evangelical imagination in profound ways. *'What exactly does it mean to know God without words?'*

And so, the seeds of my future life as a theologian were sown.

2

Formation, vocation and change

I'M NOT REALLY one for epiphanies. But I did wake up one morning in 1987 and knew that I was called to the ministry of Word and Sacrament. By 'call' I simply mean that I somehow knew (intuition?) that this was what I wanted to do and where in life I should go to next. I had enjoyed my time in nursing. I didn't have anything that I wanted to get away from. It was just the right time to move into a different vocation. At the time I couldn't really see the connection between these two vocations. However, as in all things, looking back it is easier to see. I never felt called to parish ministry. I assumed that my calling was to hospital chaplaincy. My father was a hospital chaplain (not to suggest that chaplaincy is genetic), and because of my nursing background this seemed like the obvious place for me to be located. My intention was to train for ordination in the Church of Scotland and then become a hospital chaplain. There was of course a problem. My earlier scepticism towards education caught up with me. My pattern at school was: do nothing for a year and fail your exams; realise that was a mistake and do lots for a year and pass your exams with flying colours; do nothing for a year and fail your exams; then complain that the system has failed you. That same pattern followed me through my first year in nursing until I finally wised up and got my head down. So, the first thing that I had to do in order to follow my vocation was to go back to night school and catch up on what I should have done at school. I confess that I thoroughly enjoyed that experience. Learning as an adult when you can see the point of your education is much easier than learning as a youngster who has no idea what they want from life.

So I turned up at Aberdeen University keen to learn and ready for what God had for me next. I was immediately surprised. One of the first classes I went to was a

24

Practical Theology course on pastoral care in the Parish. Here I encountered a strange revelation of my future. The basic message of the class was 'When you are doing a funeral, don't throw stones at coffins as it tends to upset relatives.' The point being that when you pick up a handful of earth to throw onto the coffin when it is laid in the grave, make sure there are no stones in it because the rattling can be disturbing for relatives and mourners. In those days Practical Theology was very much 'handy household hints for ministers'. But oddly, that was the moment I discovered my vocation to the work of Practical Theology. I don't mean to sound mystical. It's just what happened. Sometimes you just know what the right thing is to do. I left that class knowing that my future lay as a practical theologian. I completed my BD and my PhD, was ordained by the Presbyterian Church of Scotland, and worked for a few years as a hospital chaplain, before moving on into lecturing positions, first at the University of Glasgow, and then at the University of Aberdeen where I have been since 1997. My alma mater has become my home.

Formation, vocation, trust and gratitude

In the end, despite, or perhaps because of, not having a career plan, I ended up working in three different professions: nursing, ministry and university education. There are at least two things that I have learned from my vocational career. They relate to *formation* and *vocation.* You can see by the parts of my story outlined in chapter 1 that by the time I entered the academy, I had been shaped and formed in a quite particular way, and had been gifted insight and a set of questions and perspectives that those with a different formation and a different set of life experiences may not have considered. It's not that my questions and insights were any better or more important than other people's. They were however questions and insights that may not have occurred to people approaching the development of theology who have a different perspective and a different formation. I like to think of it in this way. My nursing and chaplaincy experience was my place of formation. These professions were the place where I was shaped and formed to be a certain kind of person and to see the world in a certain kind of way. When I entered the academy, my *formation* became the seedbed for my theological *vocation*: what God has called me to be and to do as a theologian.

This in turn taught me something important about the meaning of *vocation*. Sometimes we can think about vocation in the same way as we might think about a career plan: 'God has one road for me, I must find it and make sure it is the right one. It would be a disaster if I missed my vocation!' But that is not my experience. My experience is that we have a series of vocations that we fulfil over time. When I was a nurse, that was my vocation; when I was a chaplain, that was my vocation; now I am an academic, that is my vocation. Vocation stretches across the whole span of our lives. I have a vocation as a father, as a husband, as a friend, as a citizen. All these vocations together orientate me towards what God wants me to do in the world and enables me to remain faithful to the tasks that are given to me as I try to participate with God in the facilitation and actualisation of God's unending, Grace-filled neighbourly love. Vocations are often surprising (you never know quite where God will lead you next), but then God is a God of surprises. *Vocation requires that we remain in the places God wants us to be at the times God wants us to be there.* This requires an attitude of trust, thankfulness and humility. I'm not sure I always have such an attitude, but I know that it sits at the heart of what it means to walk with Jesus through the strangeness of this world.

3

Thinking about theology

HAVING LAID OUT a little of my journey into theology, I'd like now to take some time to reflect on what I think theology is and what it means to be a theologian.

Posture, position and imagination

I began this book with a personal reflection on how I became the kind of theologian that I am, partly because that is what this book series is about, but also because it is important to recognise that theology doesn't come from nowhere. Theologians don't just 'turn up' with a set of ideas. There is inevitably an element of context and to an extent, autobiography within all theologies. It may be more apparent in something like Augustine's *Confessions*,[1]

---

[1] Augustine, *Confessions* (Oxford: Oxford University Press, 1992).

31

Bonhoeffer's *Life Together*,[2] or Stanley Hauerwas's memoir *Hannah's Child*,[3] but it runs through the work of all theologians. Similarly, our own stories reveal themselves in the theologians we choose to engage with and those whom we choose not to engage with. Our stories run through our denominational preferences, the methodological choices we make (e.g. for the reasons mentioned earlier, I could never use statistical methods), the weight and significance we place on certain ideas, concepts, the intellect, human experience and so forth. Before we sit down to do the formal tasks of theology there are a multitude of factors at play which implicitly or explicitly form and guide us in our choices and decision making. We always do theology from somewhere and noticing that 'somewhere' matters.

In qualitative research we use the concept

[2] Bonhoeffer, D., Kelly, G. B., Bloesch, D. W., Burtness, J. H. and Bonhoeffer, D., *Life Together* (Minneapolis: Fortress Press, 1996).

[3] Hauerwas, Stanley, *Hannah's Child*: *A Theologian's Memoir* (London: SCM Press, 2012).

of *reflexivity* to express the need to be aware of the way in which our own stories and experiences impact upon the decisions we make in our research. Reflexivity requires that we are aware of our histories, presuppositions, assumptions, internal biases and are able to monitor intentionally why we respond (or don't respond) in certain ways and why we make certain decisions. 'Why did I choose this interpretation rather than that interpretation?' 'Why did I feel angry with this person when I don't even know them?' 'Why am I reading this as a Calvinist and not as a Methodist?' Often, we choose interpretations, concepts and perspectives because they are closer to our own desires and experiences. Likewise, we often respond, positively or negatively, to people we do not know because they remind us of people that we do know (or vice versa)! Reflexivity is a crucial tool for the qualitative researcher, but it is also a vital skill for the theologian. To be aware of the impact of our personal narratives and the complexities of our personal and corporate location and histories on the decisions we make, and the theological constructions we create, helps us to avoid constructing theology, and ultimately God, in our own image. Theological reflexivity helps us to be open to the possibility that we may be wrong (intellectual humility), that theology is always best done with an awareness of one's inner world (one's personal story, implicit biases and inner temptations), and the world around us (culture, context, world view and so forth), and how these things impact upon the work we are engaged with. The posture, position and imagination of the theologian is of great importance.

Theology as a guide on the journey

The Christian life is always a journey. We are a people who are on the move, living fully in this world, but always with an eye on the world to come. The apostle Paul puts it this way: 'But we are citizens of heaven, where the Lord Jesus Christ lives. And we are eagerly waiting for him to return as our Saviour. He will take our weak mortal bodies and change them into glorious bodies like his own, using the same power with which he will bring everything under his control' (Philippians 3:20). Our heavenly citizenship does not, of course, allow us to abrogate our earthly citizenship. Jesus tells us that our task is to do God's will on earth as it is done in heaven (Matthew 6:10) So we move through the world in ways that reveal and confirm our dual citizenship. Jesus sends us out into the world (John 17:18) on the journey of faith, but we are not left to negotiate the terrain alone. We are provided with a guide: 'I will ask the Father, and he will give you another Helper to be with you forever. The Helper is the Spirit of truth' (John 14:16-27). We are asked to navigate difficult terrain, but we are guided by the Holy Spirit in all things (John 14:26).

Theology is knowledge of God, and a guide for the journey. Our theology situates us within the story of God's redeeming movement in, to and for the world, and provides us with ideas, concepts and practices that enable us to think and to act in Christ-like ways. This of course raises the question of what exactly it might

35

mean to *know* God? God is radically unlike human beings. God is *unfathomable*: 'Can you fathom the mysteries of God? Can you probe the limits of the Almighty' (Job 11:7)? God is *immortal* and *unapproachable*: 'the blessed and only Ruler, the King of kings and Lord of lords, who alone is immortal and who lives in unapproachable light, whom no one has seen or can see' (Timothy 6:16). God is spirit: 'God is spirit, and his worshipers must worship in the Spirit and in truth (John 4:24).' God is *invisible*, but at the same time God is made visible and revealed in Jesus: 'He is the image of the invisible God, the firstborn of all creation (Colossians 1:15).' Knowing such a complex God is not something that can be achieved by using the intellect alone. In order to know God, we require *revelation*. Revelation relates to the uncovering of something that was previously hidden. Revelation is not something that we work out by ourselves using our intellect and reason. It is a gift. However, that gift still has somehow to be understood, interpreted and put into practice by limited human beings. We may have the guidance of the Holy Spirit, but our interpretations of that guidance are not infallible. And this is where things start to get complicated. Because we are humans and not God, our perceptions of revelation are inevitably ambiguous, distorted and inaccurate. As Migliore has put it:

Because all human witnesses to revelation are subject to ambiguity and distortion, it is necessary to understand the reception of revelation as a dialectical process. On the one hand, there can be no reception of the revelation of God in Christ apart from attentive and trustful reading and hearing of the witness of Scripture in company with other members of the people of God. Only in the context of the faith, prayer, proclamation, sacramental life, and service of the church does the transforming power of Jesus Christ attested by Scripture become effective for us. On the other hand, there is always a need for critical appropriation of the revelation of God in

Christ as mediated to us by Scripture and the proclamation and life of the church. Only as we enter into the new freedom in Christ that resists every form of bondage, including those that may be supported by certain elements of Scripture and church teaching, do we become active and responsible recipients of the revelation of God.[4]

Appropriating revelation is a complex dialectical process wherein the community of faith over time strives together in the power of the Spirit, to ensure that the working out of God's revelation is life bringing rather than oppressive. This is a *spiritual* task, an *intellectual* and a *practical* task.

Illumination

The spiritual task relates to the idea of *illumination.* If revelation is a Divine gift, then

[4] Migliore, Daniel L., *Faith Seeking Understanding: An Introduction to Christian Theology* (Grand Rapids: Eerdmans, 1991), p. 77.

clearly, we will require the help of the Divine to acquire it. The idea of illumination refers to the ways in which God the Holy Spirit illuminates situations and experiences in such a way as to allow us to grasp that which could not be grasped without such illumination. St Augustine describes illumination in this way:

> When we lift up our eyes to the scriptures, because the scriptures have been provided by human beings, we are lifting up our eyes to the mountains from where help will come to us. Even so, because those who wrote the scriptures were human beings, they were not shining on their own, but he was the true light who illumines everyone coming into this world (John 1:9).[5]

Some of the things God gives to us can be observed and grasped via human intellect:

[5] Augustine, *Homilies on the Gospel of John 1-40*, Boniface Ramsey (ed.), trans. Edmund Hill, vol. 12 of Part III, *The Works of Saint Augustine: A Translation for the 21st Century* (New York: New City Press, 2009)

'For since the creation of the world God's invisible qualities – his eternal power and divine nature – have been clearly seen, being understood from what has been made, so that people are without excuse' (Romans 1:20). Other aspects of God's revelation have to be received via Divine illumination. The Trinity, for example, makes no logical sense, but through the illuminating light of the Spirit human beings can at least partially grasp something of its truth and live into its implications. The resurrection makes no sense in terms of human reason and intellect, but through faith – being sure of what we hope for and certain of what we cannot see (Hebrews 11) – we can grasp something of such hidden knowledge and live into it in life-bringing ways. Faith is not a human achievement, but a gift of the illumination of the Holy Spirit (Corinthians 12:3).

Scripture also shines 'the ray of divine revelation', as Thomas Aquinas has put it,[6]

[6] *Summa Theologiae:*1.9 ad 2

which makes the knowledge of God available to human beings. Illumination enables us to see the world differently. As the Apostle Paul has put it, it transforms our minds:

> Do not conform to the pattern of this world, but be transformed by the renewing of your mind. Then you will be able to test and approve what God's will is - his good, pleasing and perfect will.

As we place Scripture and tradition in dialogue with situations and experiences, so we encounter illumination that is transformative for both theology and practice. It is because our knowledge of God is first and foremost a spiritual gift that spiritual practices such as prayer, worship, contemplation, and gratitude are all crucial tools of the Christian theologian.

Knowing God and knowing things about God

Understanding revelation is a spiritual task. But it is also an intellectual and practical task. We use our intellect to try and discern revelation via the intellectual quest. This would be the standard approach of systematic and philosophical theology. The scrupulous exploration of texts is a vital aspect of the theological task and is deeply embedded within the history of the formation of doctrine and Christian understanding. This dimension of the theological task is clearly important.

However, this intellectual task of coming to know things about God has a necessary corollary in the *practice* of knowing God. The practical quest for revelation sees knowledge of God emerging also from and within the actions we perform. One way of teasing this out is by reflecting on the difference between *knowing God* and *knowing things about* God. In James 2:18-19 the apostle says: 'Show me your faith without deeds, and I will show you my faith by my deeds. You believe that there is one God. Good! Even the demons believe that – and shudder.' Knowledge about God does not necessarily change anything. For James, knowledge of God needs to be held in tension with practices which embody that knowledge:

'Religion that God our Father accepts as pure and faultless is this: to look after orphans and widows in their distress and to keep oneself from being polluted by the world (James 1:27).' The intellectual task of doing theology – knowing things about God – is vitally important. There are things to be known about God which are vital for our lives of faith. Faith is seeking understanding, and understanding God and Jesus even in the limited ways that we can, involves the use of our intellect. However, the intellect is necessary but not sufficient for the theological task of knowing God.

Knowing God as a social practice

Walter Brueggemann draws attention to the role of practice in knowing God. He highlights the implications of Jeremiah 22:15-16:

'Does it make you a king
to have more and more cedar?
Did not your father have food and drink?
He did what was right and just,
so all went well with him.

He defended the cause of the poor and
needy,
and so all went well.
Is that not what it means to know me?'
declares the Lord.

Jeremiah here is speaking about King Josiah
whom he says is a good king. Why is he a good
king? Because he defends the poor and the
needy. The key point for current purposes is in
the last sentence '*Is that not what it means to
know me?*' Jeremiah does not say that Josiah
knows God and as a consequence goes out
and cares for the poor. *Caring for the poor is
an aspect of knowing God.* Brueggemann puts
it this way:

> Jeremiah 22:15-16 continues to be a pivot
> point in my thinking wherein 'care for the
> poor and needy' is equated by the prophet
> with 'knowledge of Yahweh.' That is, Yahweh
> is known in and through the praxis of faith
> that refuses to separate thought from action,
> body from spirit, or earth from heaven. This

44

characteristic insistence of biblical faith is so urgent in the church precisely because the church continues to be tempted by a kind of transcendentalism that removes the will and purpose of God from the 'mundane' matters of economics and politics. It is exactly that dualism that so pervades modern thought against which the Old Testament bears such powerful witness.[7]

Brueggemann offers a significant challenge to those who might desire to separate orthodoxy from orthopraxy. We come to know God as we do what pleases God. Knowing God is something we do with our minds, but it is also something we do with the whole of our bodies. It is not simply a set of ideas and concepts. It is also a fundamental orientation to God wherein knowledge emerges from and is embedded in our actions of justice, peace, friendship and fairness. As we engage in actions aimed at fairness, social justice and faithful change

[7] Brueggemann, Walter, *The Practice of Homefulness* (Cascade Books, 2014).

we are living into something of what it means to know God. Knowing things about God and knowing God are thus seen to be inextricably interlinked. We need both.

Disability and theology

This way of thinking about theology underpins much of my work in the areas of Practical Theology in general, and more specifically my work on disability and mental health. It is when we (all of us together), take time to explore the life experiences of people who are often marginalised, excluded and treated unjustly (what James and Jesus might refer to as 'the poor'), that we begin to see the importance of holding the critical tension between knowing things about God and knowing God in practice.

Take for example my early work on theology and schizophrenia in *Resurrecting the Person: Friendship and the care of people with mental health problems*.[8] There I looked

8 Swinton, John, *Resurrecting the Person: Friendship and the Care of People with Mental Health Problems* (Nashville: Abingdon Press, 2000).

at what a specifically Christian view of schizophrenia might look like. Schizophrenia is a highly stigmatised condition which is deeply impacted by the negative ways in which our culture and the media portray it – or better, mis-portray it. In that book I used the perspective of liberation theology to show the ways in which the cultural marginalisation and misrepresentation of people living with schizophrenia served to disadvantage people with this condition in profound ways. In that book I deconstructed schizophrenia, separating its clinical from its cultural constructions and showing that the deep stigma attached to this diagnosis can be devastating for people, quite apart from the particularities of their symptoms. I reconstructed schizophrenia in a theological frame that enabled the personhood and humanness of those who live with this difficult condition to throw light on precisely how the church should understand the experience theologically and respond faithfully. Whilst things like medication and therapy are important, what people require at a deeper level is simpler and more basic: *Christ-like friendship.* In John 15:15 Jesus re-names his disciples:

> I no longer call you servants, because a servant does not know his master's business. Instead, I have called you friends, for everything that I learned from my Father I have made known to you.

Within this profound act of renaming, the relationship of friendship becomes the primary form of discipleship. But what exactly do we mean by friendship? Jesus spends his time with tax collectors, sinners and prostitutes (Luke 7:34), and he offers them friendship. The friendships of Jesus are not based on similarity between people. They are not based on an exchange of social goods wherein like attracts like: 'You give me this and I'll give you that and we will remain friends. If you don't give me the social goods, I want then I don't want to be your friend.' (We might call this 'Facebook friendship'.) Rather, they are based on love, grace, acceptance, and a desire to do the best for the other (Mark 12:31). As we engage in such relationships, so we come to know Jesus more fully. True we could talk about the way in which such friendships reflect Jesus, but it is not until we engage in them that we know what they feel like and ultimately what that means. For true understanding, theory and concepts cannot be separated from the action of friendship.

Importantly and somewhat prophetically, contrary to what we often assume, Jesus did not sit with those on the margins of society. Rather, *he moved the margins.* Those engaging in the religion of the time and who rejected the marginalised, often in the name of their knowledge of God, didn't notice that and continued to think that they were worshipping God and went on living as if their knowledge was the only revelation available. Meantime, God was on 'the margins' shifting the centre and offering friendship. The social location of Jesus reveals the proper social location of the church and the primary orientation of the theological journey. Critical theological reflection on the experience of schizophrenia thus reveals a fundamental Christian practice that in turn discloses the nature and social location of God: with the poor and the outcast. This liberative realisation that God is revealed in text and in human relationships has been a crucial aspect of my theological development over the years. It has also been formative for me in terms of the kinds of methods that I have developed and used, particularly in relation to the use of qualitative research as a way of doing theology.

4

Practical theology
and qualitative research

IN 2006, MY COLLEAGUE Harriet Mowat and I wrote a book imaginatively titled *Practical Theology and Qualitative Research.* There we explored some of the ways in which theologians can effectively and faithfully utilise qualitative research as an aspect of theological enquiry. Building on that work over the years I have been involved in the development of the area of empirical theological research that has come to be known as Theological Ethnography. Theological Ethnography is a way of utilising qualitative research methods for theological ends. The term 'ethnography' is used in a very loose and all-encompassing way to refer to any kind of qualitative research. Theological Ethnography is distinct from social scientific approaches to the study of religion. It does not attempt to scrutinise and analyse religion as a purely human behavioural phenomenon. It takes the presence of God as a given reality. In other words, it does not seek to bracket out God and the spiritual from the empirical research process. Instead, it seeks to generate a theological attitude towards empirical methods that views them as participants in the theological quest. Although it emerges from Practical Theology, Theological Ethnography remains in some senses distinct from certain methodological strands in that it is both theological and empirical without being correlational. In other words, it does not structure the relationship between social science and theology as stages in a correlated conversation.[9] Whereas a correlative approach

[9] The theoretical groundwork for Theological Ethnography can be found in Swinton, J. and Mowat, H., *Practical Theology and Qualitative Research* (SCM, 2nd Edition, 2016), Ward, P. (ed.), *Perspectives in Ecclesiology and Ethnography* (Grand Rapids: Eerdmans, 2012), Ward, P. 'Ecclesiology and Ethnography with Humility: Going Through Barth' in *Studia Theologica*, July (2016). Murray, P. 'Searching the Living Truth of The Church in Practice: On the Transformative Task of Systematic Theology' in *Modern Theology* 30.2 2014. Scharen, C. and Vigen, A.M. (eds.) *Ethnography as Christian Theology and Ethics* (London: Bloomsbury, 2011).

might begin by doing social scientific research and then correlate the findings with theology, Theological Ethnography sees the beginning point of all research as residing within the fact that we live in a Created order. Put slightly differently, everything begins with God. If we are looking at psychiatry, social care, politics or economics, we assume that these things occur within God's creation. In this way Theological Ethnography in a sense re-enchants the world, assuming that God's work is not confined to history or the realm of the religious.

That is not to suggest that the researcher assumes they have Divine knowledge that everyone has to listen and adhere to! For the reasons stated previously, revelation is a complicated thing to work out and theologians using ethnography as an aspect of their theological reflections must recognise the significance of sin, fallenness and the tendency of human beings to create God in their own image. This is why Theological Ethnography like all theology, should be *critical*, dialogical and intellectually humble. The key point is that Theological Ethnography begins with the assumption of the possibility of God and that theology is a vital part of its empirical enquiry.

This approach shifts attention in theology from a focus solely on abstract forms of reasoning, towards the various ways in which theology is situated within the lived experience of communities and individuals. It assumes that alongside of reflection on what God has done in the past, theological exploration of what God is doing in the present is important. Theological Ethnography is a way in which researchers can potentially examine *living theology* (theology as it is lived out and lived into), as an indication and signification of the presence and actions of God. Theological Ethnography opens the possibility of clearly, critically, and carefully attending to the ways in which the presence of God is experienced by particular individuals and religious communities and the ways in which that presence affects and impacts upon our knowledge of God.

We might think of it in this way. Theological Ethnography relates closely to systematic and philosophical theology in that it takes seriously doctrinal and systematic forms of knowledge and reasoning but does so in combination with empirical methods of enquiry. In the same way as, one might explore the writings of Augustine, Cone, Lacugna or Barth with care and critical rigour, in order to understand the nature of God's revelation and what that means for human beings, Theological Ethnography uses a variety of exploratory approaches to examine critically the text of Christian people and communities as they interact with and impact upon the texts of the world. The theology that is learned through this process is not simply returned to the academy and assessed by what we think we have already come to know via intellectual theological reflection (although exploring issues around orthodoxy is an important part of the process). The exegesis of Christian life is granted a degree of autonomy with the possibility of illuminating and enlightening our understanding of who God is and what such knowledge means for the practice of knowing God within both church and world.

Theology and mental health

An example of what this looks like can be found in the phenomenological qualitative research that I carried out for my book: *Finding Jesus in the Storm: The spiritual lives of Christians with mental health challenges*.[10] Using a phenomenological approach[11] I tried to put to one side assumptions about what certain mental health challenges were (schizophrenia, bipolar disorder and major depression) as conceived through standard clinical and theological frameworks and assumptions, and to explore the mental health experiences of Christians *as they were lived.*

One of the problems for individuals living with mental health challenges is that people tend to think of them in very thin ways. By that I mean that if a person receives a diagnosis

[10] Swinton, John, *Finding Jesus in the Storm: The Spiritual Lives of Christians with Mental Health Challenges* (Grand Rapids: Eerdmans, 2020).

[11] By this I mean an approach that intentionally puts to one side the assumptions that one has about a phenomenon and seeks to see the thing in itself before we develop eternal theoretical frameworks and perspectives.

of say schizophrenia, that is pretty much all anyone seems to see after that. Such narrowing of personhood is the essence of stigma. Stigma is the enemy of community and the destroyer of the possibility of friendship. The fact that people have a name, a history, that they love, cry, have hopes and dreams for now and the future is reduced to a thin description of what people think other people should be like. A phenomenological approach helps us to get past thin descriptions and move towards thick descriptions[12] which really see people in all of their complexity. When we do this important theological and practical issues bubble up to the surface. Take for instance the experience of depression.

Depression

Central to living with depression is the painful experience of darkness, abandonment and a sense of alienation. Sometimes that alienation is felt as distance from God as well as others

[12] A description that takes account of feelings, emotions, interpretations, context, culture and so forth.

and self. People feel abandoned. It is often reported that some Christians have certain theodicies (explanations for the presence of evil and suffering in the light of God's love and power) that they use to explain experiences such as depression. So, people will say things like: 'You must have done something wrong for God to punish you like this!' 'If you just had enough faith you wouldn't feel that way!' 'You must find that hidden sin ...' Such explanations are not only unhelpful, they are also inaccurate.

A spirituality of abandonment

In beginning to explore how and why such casual theodicies might be misleading and destructive, Theological Ethnography begins by listening carefully to what people say about the actual experience of depression. The process involves deep reflective interviews that explore not what depression is, but what it *means* to be depressed, or more accurately what it means to be a Christian and to be depressed. In this way the theological questions emerge from the ground up rather than from the top down. An example will help draw out this point.

David lives with enduring depression. One of the most distressing aspects of his depression is the sense that he is separated from and abandoned by God:

> If you can't feel the presence of God then that's ... throughout Scripture the presence of God is considered the rock, you know, that's your foundation. I mean from Job to Jeremiah to what Christ talks about, and if you can't have that it's really disenchanting, it's really bewildering.

David has spoken to people in his church community about this and has had several negative responses similar to those mentioned above. David's experience raises the crucial question of what we mean when we talk about God's presence or God's absence.

Once the question has been raised, we can allow it to orientate our reflections on and interpretations of Scripture. When we turn to

Scripture, we find an unusual and sometimes overlooked tension. On the one hand God promises to be with us at all times and forever: 'For the LORD your God is a merciful God; he will not abandon or destroy you or forget the covenant with your forefathers, which he confirmed to them by oath' (Deuteronomy 4:31). And yet elsewhere we find something else: 'Truly you are a God who has been hiding himself, the God and Saviour of Israel' (Isaiah 45:15). How can God be present and absent at the same time? The answer of course is that we don't know. It is a mystery. But it is a mystery that reveals something important. The sense of abandonment and separation from God that people with depression often feel, is not alien to our tradition and is not inevitably linked to sin. Indeed, it is an important part of our personal and corporate spirituality.

A focus on the psalms of lament quickly draws attention to the common human experience of a deep sense of abandonment. There are more psalms of lament than any other form of psalm. God has given us a worshipful language to use when we are faced with suffering and abandonment. Sometimes the psalmist's suffering and sense of abandonment is resolved (Psalm 13) At other times it just hangs there unanswered: 'Darkness is my only companion ...' (Psalm 88). However, we must remember that even though his cry is bleak, the psalmist is still talking to God. The problem is not that he has lost his faith. The problem is that he has lost his sense of *connection* with God. This of course is precisely what many people with depression experience. As Jennifer put it in my interview with her: 'I do cry to God. But I just can't find him. Maybe it's me?' Reflection on the psalms of lament would indicate that it is not 'just her.' The experience of disconnection is part of our spirituality as it is laid out in the psalms; the prayerbook of the bible as Bonhoeffer has put it.[13]

If we then turn to Jesus's cry of abandonment from the cross 'My God, My

[13] Bonhoeffer, Dietrich, Kelly, Geffrey B., Bloesch, Daniel W., Burtness, James H., *Prayerbook of the Bible* (Minneapolis: Fortress Press, 1996).

63

God. Why have you forsaken me (Matthew 27:46)', another important dimension of the experience of abandonment is revealed. Jesus, the image of the invisible God (Colossians 1:15), experiences God's abandonment. Gone is the warm language of 'Abba father' that he used earlier in his life. Now God is distant, unhearing. Jesus is abandoned. The one who is without sin finds himself feeling abandoned by God.

There are many things to be learned from this experience, but for current purposes we are reminded that even when God seems distant or even absent, Jesus remains with us and shares deeply even in our pain and feelings of alienation. Abandonment and a sense of disconnection from God need not be seen as an indication of personal sin or a lack of faithfulness; such a sense of abandonment is a part of our Christian spirituality. Noticing such theological insights will not take away the pain of depression, but it does assure us that such a sense of darkness and abandonment is not something that is outside the history and experiences of God's people. People suffer enough without the ascription of forms of spiritual stigma that stand at odds with God's loving presence and the apparent absence of God that we encounter in scripture.

This brief reflection helps us to see the approach and the potential of Theological Ethnography for bringing new questions to the theological table and developing fresh insights and understandings of Scripture and tradition that can help us in the complex process of understanding the revelation that has been given to us. This idea of bringing new questions to the theological table brings us to the final aspect of my theology that I want to share in this book: *the theology of disability.*

5

Theology and Disability: Who gets to ask the theological questions?

SITTING AT THE HEART of a good deal of my theology are the life experiences of people living with disabilities, or more specifically people living with intellectual disabilities and people living with dementia. My time working alongside people with such life experience, coupled with the insights I have gained over the years from friends who have dementia and intellectual disability, has placed the area of disability theology firmly on my horizon.

I have always been fascinated by the question of who it is that gets to ask questions in the theological conversations that go on as we wrestle with God's revelation. Traditionally the questions that gain most attention are raised by academics and worked out within the academy. These questions can be fruitful and enlightening, but I've always had a nagging concern that there were certain questions that were not being brought into the conversation. One of the things I try to do as a Practical Theologian is to attempt to allow the questions that emerge from the experience of disability to enter into dialogue with the questions (and answers) that emerge from other forms of theological discussion. Qualitative research methods have been important in allowing people with intellectual disabilities to talk for themselves about issues relating to spirituality.[14] Such research brings crucial questions and issues to the fore. The following conversation with Elaine illustrates something of this approach:

> Interviewer: Where do you feel you belong?
> Elaine: Well I sort of feel I'm trying to help in the community. I'm participating.
> Interviewer: You're trying to help within this community.

[14] Swinton, J, *A space to listen. Learning Disability Practice* 5 (2), 6-7, 2002. Swinton, J., and Powrie, E., *Why are we here? Understanding the spiritual lives of people with learning disabilities* (London: Mental Health Foundation, 2004).

Elaine: Well this area here: I'm trying to
build up a friendship.

Interviewer: You're trying to build up
friendship. Where is that happening?

Elaine: At the church.

Interviewer: At the church, and how are
you getting on there?

Elaine: OK.

Interviewer: Is that by meeting people or by
them inviting you into their homes ... or?

Elaine: By meeting people at the church
and in the home.

Interviewer: And how do you find that? Do
you find it easy or difficult?

Elaine: Easy.

Interviewer: Quite easy. So do you go to
meetings during the week or do you
go to people's houses or do you just
see them at mass?

Elaine: Just see them at mass.

(Swinton and Powrie, 2004, p. 32)

Reflection on Elaine's story indicates her
need for friendship and belonging and how the

church can be a source of meeting that need. However, the kind of friendship that is often offered is limited to the Sunday service. Elaine desires Christ-like friendship. What she gets is a Sunday-only friendship. The questions raised here are: what does it mean for the Body of Christ (the community of the friends of Jesus) only to offer limited friendship to people with intellectual disabilities? What causes such limited hospitality? These questions take us into an exploration of the nature of Christian hospitality, the friendships of Jesus and the expectation that the Body of Christ is a lived reality rather than a nice idea.

Knowing God

One of my primary foci has been on the lives of those with profound intellectual disabilities and people living with advanced dementia. People with these life experiences cannot articulate questions directly, but their lives do raise profound theological issues. My work with people with mild intellectual disability (like Elaine above), could be described in terms of enabling and empowering people to participate in the theological conversation. My work with people with profound intellectual disabilities and those living with brain damage such as dementia is probably best considered as a form of *theological advocacy*. Advocacy involves speaking out on behalf of another individual or a group of individuals who cannot speak directly for themselves in a way that represents their best interests. Theological advocacy means using one's theological skills and knowledge to enable people to be accurately represented within the theological discourse and the practices of the church. Stephen Post[15] has spoken about the dangers of hypercognition for people with advanced dementia. He suggests that we live in a hypercognitive society which can be toxic for people with dementia. Hypercognition occurs when an individual or a society places

[15] Post, Stephen G., *The Moral Challenge of Alzheimer Disease: Ethical Issues from Diagnosis to Dying*, second edition (Balitimore: Johns Hopkins University Press, 2000).

more emphasis on issues relating to intellect, reason, productivity, competitiveness and power than on things like love, community, good relationship and human flourishing. In a world that has come to worship the intellect, having a condition within which the intellectual acuity is either not present or is slipping away has a very sharp and negative cultural connotation. If our intellect is central to what we are as meaningful human beings, then how are we to view those who are either losing or have never had this faculty? This kind of concern lurks beneath many of the discussions on prenatal testing for disability and euthanasia for people with dementia.[16]

Transfer that malignant cultural hypercognition into a theological context and you discover people asking questions such as, 'If this person can't proclaim Jesus with their mouths as Paul states, how can they be saved?'

[16] Macadam, J. Interview with Mary Warnock: 'A duty to die?', *Life and Work*, 25 (October, 2008). Acharya, K. *Prenatal testing for intellectual disability: misperceptions and reality with lessons from Down's syndrome* (Developmental Disabilities Research Reviews 17(1): 27–31 (2011).

'How can this person take the sacrament when they don't know what they are doing?' Or, as one gentleman at an engagement party in Australia recently informed me: 'If I am deemed to be incompetent in my job as an accountant because I can no longer count, isn't it pretty obvious that someone becomes spirituality incompetent when they can no longer remember Jesus?' What we encounter here is a hypercognitive theology that matches the expectations of a hypercognitive society, only this time it is not your life that people think should be taken from you, it's your salvation. Even though people with severe intellectual disability and advanced dementia cannot articulate questions, their presence certainly seems to.

Being in Christ

This is why theological advocacy is so important. Theological advocacy stands against such destructive views and seeks to present an alternative both in terms of theory and practice It's not a matter of speaking *for* people in a kind of paternalistic way. It's about speaking *against* theologies and structures that deliberately or otherwise cause harm and misrepresent God and the nature of human beings. If we pick up on the logic of hypercognitive theologies, we can see the importance of such advocacy. The inference is that salvation emerges via our intellectual ability and cognitive capacity. It raises the rather odd question: just how much do people think you need to know about Jesus before your salvation is retained or slips way? Such a perspective also makes everyone's salvation insecure. Imagine standing at the top of a flight of stairs. You trip and fall down the stairs and sustain severe brain damage. At the top of the stairs, you are a disciple, but by the time you reach the bottom you are not! It would be a rather fickle God who treated us in such ways. So how best can we advocate for a different way of thinking and approaching such issues?

In 2 Corinthians 5:17 Paul says: Therefore, if anyone is in Christ, he is a new creation. The old has passed away; behold, the new has come.' As Christians we no longer find our identity in what we have done, what we can do or what we cannot do. Our identity is found in Christ. Who we are is to an extent, a mystery to us. Our identity is hidden in Christ: 'For you died, and your life is now hidden with Christ in God (Colossians 3:3).' It may well be that we forget things or we cannot understand things, but that does not impact upon who we are in Christ. It is not *our* memory that counts but God's. God never forgets us:

> Can a mother forget the baby at her breast
> and have no compassion on the
> child she has borne?
> Though she may forget,
> I will not forget you. (Isaiah 49:15)

We may not know many things, but our knowledge is not the basis for God's love. We may not remember many things, but God's memory will not let us go. Theological advocacy in this situation moves us beyond hypercognition, insecurity and anxiety, and reorientates us towards a God who is faithful, loving, kind and ever-present. It is that God that has always been the focus of my theology and it is that God whom I have spent many years trying to understand and live well with.

Conclusion:
Walking with Jesus
in 'Strange' places

IN THIS BOOK I have tried to give you a sense of what theology is for me, how I go about doing it and why I think it is an important enterprise for church and world. I am sure I get things wrong sometimes, which is why critical, hospitable conversation is vital for me as it is for all effective theological development. Working out and living into God's revelation is not an easy task. However, the kinds of ideas and approaches that I have laid out in this book give some insight into the tools for the journey that I have used over the years. Despite all of the challenges, I remain optimistic about the future of the church universal, as long as it remains faithful to its task to care for strangers, love the outcast and offer hospitality to those who face fear and anxiety in what is often a deeply inhospitable world.

The key of course is love. Towards the

beginning of Michael Verdie's recent powerful film *Love is Listening: Dementia Without Loneliness*, an African American woman with advanced dementia reflects on her life experience. 'I don't know where I am. I don't know where I'm going. I don't know where I've just come from. But I'm not fearful.' She pauses and looks deeply into the eyes of the person she is talking to. 'Because I see all around me - I don't see a lot - but I see patience.' She looks upwards and away, her eyes glaze over a little. 'I see gratitude. I see tolerance.' She slowly looks back towards her friend and smiles. 'I think I see love.' She smiles. 'And your face is a picture of love.'

It's a very beautiful and moving scene. Even when we feel lost, uncertain about the future; unable to work out where life is going, we can still feel, see and experience love. More than that, the presence of such love can drive out fear. The experience of dementia, at times, can be quite frightening. We need people who will love us out of our fear and help us to find love amidst the challenges. If we know we are loved, we need not be fearful. In the time of dementia (like all times), we need people who will act gently, patiently, kindly, humbly, respectfully, peacefully. We need people whose lives are filled with forgiveness, honesty and integrity (1 Corinthians 13). We need to be reminded of the presence of the God who is love. We need people whose faces are a picture of love.

I'll leave the last word to Alice, one of the participants in the mental health project I mentioned earlier in the book. Alice lives with schizophrenia and has been in and out of hospital on many occasions. Being hospitalised is not an ideal way to find community, and yet:

> When I was in hospital, I met some really interesting people. I met Jesus at one point; he's a fifty-year-old mouldy man from London. Being Jesus seems to be a common mental health issue; it's really interesting. But, yeah, he was Jesus or an Old Testament prophet; [it] depended on the day. But I met a guy in his sixties who thought I was his mum. And I met a

whole lot of interesting people. I met a lady who thought her face was falling off and all this kind of stuff. It's so fascinating what people's brains can do to them. It's just ... and I think for all of us, because we were all in it together, there's a sense of community that is definitely I find I've missed, a lot. And we're the nuttiest community out there, and we used to just sit around in a 138 circle and smoke up a storm and swear and drink and whatever, but we understood there was no need to explain if you start talking to a corner. Everyone would just go, 'Ah, she's off her meds again!' No one would care! There was a real sense of family. And I haven't found that again.[17]

The thing that troubles me about Alice's story of finding acceptance in her strange community is that someone who loves Jesus can't seem to find friends within the community of the friends of Jesus. I wonder why that is?

[17]   Swinton, J., *Finding Jesus in the Storm*, p. 158.